The Wanna Beez

Christine Dawe

Published in 2004 by:
Nelson Thornes Ltd
Delta Place
27 Bath Road
CHELTENHAM
GL53 7TH
United Kingdom

04 05 06 07 08 / 10 9 8 7 6 5 4 3 2 1

A catalogue record for this book is available from the British Library

ISBN 0-7487-9011-X

Cover illustration by Tony Forbes
Page make-up by Tech-Set, Gateshead

Printed in Croatia by Zrinski

Contents

A play in 3 acts for 6 to 8 parts.

Cast in order of appearance

Alex	A day-dreamer and often a few steps behind the others
Ben	A joker
Carol	A show-off who likes to be the centre of attention
Mel	A moaner
Ben's dad	He runs a pub and is always busy
Presenter	A voice over the loud speaker
Vic	The bartender at the pub
Kelly Matthews	A TV star

Non-speaking Parts

Cleaner
Security man
Little old lady

[Ben's dad and Presenter can be played by the same person]

[Vic and Kelly Matthews can be played by the same person]

Act 1

4 parts: Alex
          Ben
          Caroline
          Mel

Scene: The stage of Sheldon Village Hall. A group of friends have just finished a rehearsal of their new number. The hall is empty. There is a small table with a flask and mugs on it.

Alex is strumming on a guitar. Ben is flicking through a pop magazine.

Carol is brushing her hair and wearing knee socks with black and white stripes.

Mel is packing away the drums.

Alex	Wow. That was great!
Ben	Yeah. I'm sure we're ready now for our first gig.
Carol	But where?
Mel	Who will give us a chance? No one.
Alex	How can we get into show biz?
Mel	We'll never hit the big time. It's hopeless.
Carol	And what shall we call ourselves?
Alex	We've got to have a name.

Ben	Then we can get an agent.
Alex	A what?
Ben	An agent.
Alex	What, like James Bond?
Mel	Not a secret agent! Someone to help us to get gigs.
Ben	Or make a demo tape, or a demo CD.
Carol	Right. Let's think of a really good name.
Alex	Something catchy.
Mel	Something easy to remember.
Ben	Something with style.
Mel	That trips off the tongue.
Carol	Like the Candy Girls. They're great.
Ben	Or Blue 4 Boyze. They're even better.
Mel	Or The Chat Room.
Alex	The who?
Mel	No. Not 'The Who'. Only grandads remember 'The Who'.
Ben	The Chat Room. They're good. They're the new band.
Carol	Oooh, yes. I love The Chat Room. They're great.
Mel	But it's OK for them. They've already made it. We're still wannabes.

Alex	Wannabees? Aren't they like kangaroos?
Mel	Not wallabies! Wannabees. It means 'want to be'. We *want to be* great.
Carol	That's it! We'll call ourselves 'The Wanna Bees'.
Alex	The what?
Carol	The Wanna Bees. Bees, with a double ee in the middle. You know. Bees. Buzz – Buzz – Buzz. Bees!
Alex	What are you going on about?
Carol	Or we could put a letter Z on the end of Bees and spell it The Wanna Beez. Just to make it different. To make it buzzzzzzzz!
Ben	Oh yeah. Like The Beatles.
Alex	What do you mean?
Ben	Well, bees are insects, aren't they? And beetles are insects when they're spelt with a double 'ee'.
Carol	But The Beatles didn't spell their name with a double ee, did they?
Mel	They changed the spelling to 'Beatles' with ea. 'Beat' is the sound. Like when I beat on the drums.
Ben	Yeah. The beat of the music. The tempo. The rhythm.

Mel	So people remembered the name Beatles because it wasn't spelt right.
Carol	I see what you mean. Like Abba, with a back-to-front B in the middle. It's different. So people remember it.
Alex	Right! So, if we call ourselves The Wanna Beez, people will remember our name.
Ben	Yeah. Wanna is short for 'want to'. And we 'want to' be in show biz.
Mel	Want to be's. Wanna Beez! I like it. It's easy to say and easy to remember.
Carol	Wanna Beez? Wanna Beez? Mmm. It's not bad, but I'm not sure.
Alex	We couldn't have a name like The Candy Girls or Blue 4 Boyz.
Ben	True. We're mixed!
Alex	Are bees boys or girls?
Mel	They're mixed. There's lots of boy drones and boy workers and one girl queen bee.
Carol	Queen bee? Oh I like that. Can I be the queen bee of our band? I fancy myself as a queen bee.
Ben	Well buzz off, then!
Alex	Yeah, how about The Wanna Beez? It sounds good.

Carol	O.K. That's it then. The Wanna Beez it is. With me as Queen Bee. That's my new name. No more Carol. Just Queen Bee. Right?
Ben	OK, honey! Ha – get it? Bee . . . honey . . .
Mel	OK. If it makes you happy. What ever turns you on, babe.
Carol	Not Babe. Queenie. Queenie Queen Bee. I fancy myself as a Queen Bee.
Alex	Good. Because no-one else will fancy you in those socks.
Carol	Ooh, I can just see myself on the front of all the Pop magazines. Don't you think I look dead glam?
Alex	Glam?
Ben	More glum than glam!
Alex	What's 'glam'?
Carol	Glamorous. Trendy. Smart. Cool. Sexy.
Ben	No way. In those black and white socks, you look like a zebra. You can be on the front of a zoo magazine.
Carol	I think they look very snazzy. I've got six pairs of these at home.
Ben	Six Sox? That's a good name for a band!

Mel	You should have them in yellow and black if you're the Queen Bee?
Carol	Hey, yeah. And a stripy top. And black and yellow hair!
Alex	Anyway, why do you need six pairs?
Carol	One for every day of the week!
Ben	I'll give you some more for Christmas, Carol. Ha – get it? Christmas carol!
Alex	One for every day of the week? There are seven days in the week.
Carol	I stay in bed on Sundays! [*Carol pours out drinks for everyone.*]
Alex	Pooh! This drink smells weird. What is it? Tea or coffee?
Carol	Bovril.
Mel	I only drink fruit tea.
Carol	Beggars can't be choosers.
Alex	That sounds like the name of a band, too!
Carol	No – we'll stick with The Wanna Beez. It's got a good ring to it.
Ben	Or a good *sting* to it! Get it?
Alex	No. Sting is years old.
Ben	Never mind, Alex. Look, we've got to get an agent, who knows an agent?

Mel	Anybody know an agent? [*She looks at Alex*] Apart from 007.
	[*Silence*]
Carol	Not me.
Alex	Not me.
Mel	Not me.
Ben	Well . . .
Everyone	Yes?
Ben	Well, my dad might know one.
Mel	How?
Ben	Well . . . at his pub . . .
Everyone	Yes?
Ben	At his pub, they sometimes have karaoke nights. And a long time ago they used to have talent nights.
Mel	So?
Alex	It sounds a bit cheesy.
Ben	But there might be somebody who knows about agents or gigs or demo tapes or CDs or something.
Carol	Talent, eh? Well, why can't we be local talent and do a gig without an agent?
Mel	Because I can't go into pubs, that's why.

Alex	Well, anyway, Ben, you could ask your dad if he ever serves anybody from show biz in his pub. Can you text him now?
Ben	I forgot my mobile.
Mel	A fat lot of good you are!
Carol	Just talk to him and tell him all about The Wanna Beez and ask him if he can help in any way. Tell him I'm the Queen of The Wanna Beez.
Ben	OK. I'll try. You've really got a bee in your bonnet about that!
Carol	Hey, yeah! I'll wear a yellow and black stripy crown. All part of my new image. I'll look cool on Top of the Pops.
Alex	This is great. We're really on our way now.
Carol	[*Carol picks up a magazine and fans herself*] Look. What's this?
	[*Silence*]
Alex	Don't know.
Mel	Don't know.
Ben	What is it?
Carol	It's my first fan! [*Everyone groans*]

Act 2

3 parts: Ben
          Ben's Dad
          Vic the bartender

Scene: Inside an empty pub, day-time. There is only dim light coming in through a window. Ben's Dad is counting the mixers to see how many are left on the shelf. Then he writes down how many he needs to re-order.

Dad   Twenty-five, twenty-six, twenty-seven fizzy spritzers left on the shelf.

Ben   Good title for a song!

Dad   So that means that we've only sold three apple fizzy spritzers.

Ben   Dad?

Dad   We had thirty cans and we've still got twenty-seven left.

Ben   I thought fizzy spritzers were popular.

Dad   So did I. Oh well, I won't bother to order any more fizzy spritzers.

Ben   Dad?

Dad   Now what about the bitter lemons? And the breezers?

Ben   Dad?

Dad	Ten left on the shelf. So I need to order twenty more.
Ben	Pop?
Dad	No. We don't need any pop. We've got plenty of pop.
Ben	No, Pop, I mean you. Have you got a minute to spare?
Dad	Mmmm? What is it?
Ben	Well . . .
Dad	Do you want some pop for a party? Or some cokes?
Ben	No, Pop. It's not that.
Dad	Some crisps? What flavour? Cheese and onion? Smoky bacon?
Ben	No, it's not that.
Dad	I can tell you want something. You only call me Pop when you want something. I bet you want to borrow a fiver.
Ben	No, Pop. It's not that. But, Dad . . .
Dad	Pass the empties, will you, Ben?
Ben	Pop!
Dad	In fact, make yourself useful and wash a few while you're there.
Ben	Pop!

[*Enter Vic*]

Vic	Morning Mr Blackwell.
Dad	Morning Vic.
Vic	Morning Ben.
Ben	Hi-ya.
Dad	No. Not Hi-ya. Never mind Hi-ya. That's not what you say.
Ben	What do I say?
Dad	'Good morning' is what you say. Or better still, 'Good morning and how are you today?'
Vic	Fine, thank you, Mr Blackwell. How are you?
Dad	No, no, no. I'm not saying, 'Good morning. How are you today?' Ben is saying, 'Good morning. How are you today?'
Vic	Oh, sorry. It's so dark in here. I couldn't tell who was speaking. Good morning, Ben.
Ben	Hi-ya.
Dad	I give up!
Vic	Your voice was just like your dad's. You've got a very grown-up voice now.
Ben	Dad! Will you listen to me?
Dad	Of course I will, son. You know I'll listen to you any time. Have you finished washing those empties yet?

14

Vic	Shall I empty the ash trays, Mr Blackwell?
Dad	Yes, please. And wipe over the tables, will you?
Vic	I'll just pop out and get a damp cloth.
	[*Vic goes out*]
Ben	Dad, you know when you have karaoke nights?
Dad	Mmm.
Ben	Do people listen properly to the singers?
Dad	Mmm? I need more beer mats.
Ben	Like you always listen properly!
Dad	Eh? I'm listening. I always listen. What did you say?
Ben	Do people listen properly to the singers?
Dad	Not properly, son. They just keep on drinking and talking.
Ben	Do the singers have agents?
Dad	No way. People just pop up and grab the mike. And start singing.
Ben	Oh.
Dad	Well, *they* call it singing. More like cats in pain, I think.
	[*Vic comes back in*]
Vic	These dish cloths have seen better days.
Ben	Do you ever have talent nights?

Dad	No, not these days, son.
Vic	We tried it a few times, years ago.
Dad	But there wasn't enough talent around to keep it going.
Vic	We started with prize money.
Dad	But no one was good enough to win a prize.
Vic	We lost a lot of customers after that fire-eater. He sneezed in the gents and set light to the paper towels.
Ben	What did they do? At the talent nights?
Dad	Well, one bloke played the piano a bit.
Vic	And another had a dog that howled 'God Save the Queen'.
Dad	But I don't call that talent.
Vic	What about the woman with the snakes and doves?
Ben	What did she do?
Vic	Well, she made the doves come out of people's pockets and they flew around the bar.
Dad	Nasty, dirty things they were, too.
Vic	By the end of the night, the bar was covered in bird droppings.
Dad	There was a direct hit in the peanuts.

Ben	What did she do with the snakes?
Vic	She made them come out of a big laundry basket.
Ben	How?
Vic	She charmed them with a flute or a recorder or something.
Dad	Clarinet it was. Jazz clarinet.
Vic	Well, clarinet then. Something like that.
Dad	Dressed up in fancy dress, she was.
Vic	Like a belly dancer.
Dad	It was just a frilly nightdress with her undies showing through.
Ben	What did she do with the snakes when they were out of the basket?
Vic	Oh, they swayed about a bit, in time with the music.
Dad	Then they wound themselves around her and hissed at all the people in the bar.
Ben	Then what?
Vic	Nothing. That was the end of the act.
Dad	It *should* have been the end of the act, you mean!
Vic	Well, usually it was the end of the act.
Dad	Until that fateful night.

Ben	What fateful night?
Vic	Well, one night, Zelda, that's what she called herself, Zelda.
Dad	But her real name was Lizzy Sidebottom. She worked in the Co-op.
Vic	Well, anyway, Lizzy or Zelda or Mrs Silly Bottom, whatever she called herself, had a cold.
Dad	It was so bad, she couldn't breathe properly through her nose.
Vic	So she made a mess of playing the flute.
Dad	Clarinet. Jazz clarinet.
Vic	Clarinet, then.
Ben	What happened to the snakes?
Vic	Well, she couldn't play the flute properly.
Dad	Clarinet.
Vic	Because every time she tried to play, her nose got blocked up and the notes came out all wrong.
Dad	The sound was awful. Like cats in pain.
Ben	Everything sounds like cats in pain, to you, Dad.
Dad	That's what it was. Cats in pain. Screeching and howling. I felt like chucking a bucket of water over her.

Ben	Wow! In her frilly nightie?
Vic	Anyway, Mrs Silly Bottom was fat, forty and frumpy.
Ben	What happened to the snakes?
Vic	Well, the music was so bad, the snakes didn't know what to do.
Dad	So they started to slither all around the bar.
Vic	People were screaming and jumping on tables.
Dad	Sounded like cats in pain.
Vic	Drinks got knocked over.
Dad	Glasses got broken.
Vic	Chairs fell over.
Dad	Peanuts flew all over the place. So did bird droppings.
Vic	People hid in the corner.
Dad	Mrs Silly Bottom kept playing louder and louder.
Vic	Sounded like cats in pain.
Ben	Oh, don't you start!
Dad	And then the doves got out of their cage.
Ben	What happened to the snakes?
Dad	One slid up a woman's leg.

Vic	She had a fit. Screamed the place down.
Ben	Don't tell me. She sounded like a cat in pain!
Dad	Right.
Vic	It was worse than that.
Ben	What sounds worse than a cat in pain?
Dad	Two cats in pain.
Ben	What happened to the doves?
Dad	The snakes ate them.
Vic	Feathers went everywhere.
Dad	All in the peanuts.
Vic	And then the police arrived.
Dad	They were no use. Policewomen. They screamed the place down.
Vic	Sounded like three cats in pain.
Ben	What happened to Mrs Silly Bottom?
Vic	She stopped playing. She grabbed all the snakes and put them in the basket.
Dad	She slammed the lid on and ran out through the door in her nightdress.
Ben	Why did she have a door in her nightdress?
Dad	You what?
Ben	It's a joke. So that was the end of Zelda, was it?

Vic	She jumped into her van and raced away into the night.
Dad	We never saw her again. Nor did the Co-op.
Vic	I heard she ran off with a tattoo artist.
Dad	I wouldn't be a bit surprised.
Ben	I bet he had designs on her!
Vic	Sorry, Ben?
Ben	Get it? Tattoo artist. He had designs . . .. Oh, never mind.
Vic	So that was the end of the talent nights.
Dad	Good job, too. People didn't drink enough when the acts were on.
Vic	But a lot of glasses got broken.
Dad	And we've still got all these fizzy spritzers left. I don't know how we're going to get rid of them.
Ben	Dad?
Dad	Yes, son?
Ben	Pop, can I talk to you?
Dad	No, not now, son. I've got to open up the pub now. Some other time, eh? Pass me those empties, will you son? [*Ben groans*] Don't do that. You sound like . . . . . .
Ben	A cat in pain?

Alex	Well, did you ask him or not?
Ben	I tried. I tried. Honestly, I really tried.
Carol	Well?
Ben	But he wouldn't listen. He just didn't seem to understand what I was trying to say.
Alex	Why didn't he understand you?
Mel	Did you say it in Spanish or something?
Ben	No. Of course not!
Mel	Well, why didn't he understand you then?
Ben	Because he's my Dad! That's why. Adults never understand anything. Zero. Ziltch. That's what they understand.
Carol	That's true. They live in a world of their own. Danger! Warning! Do not enter. Adult zone. Zombies only.
Mel	My mum doesn't even understand about chat rooms or text messages or glitter lip-stick or anything.
Alex	I don't understand about glitter lip-stick!
Ben	It's good to kiss!
Carol	Oooh! Who have you been kissing?
Mel	My mum doesn't even try to learn. She's hopeless. She's a zombie.
Alex	Well, what are we going to do then?

Mel	All that hard work for nothing.
Carol	We've worked for weeks and weeks and weeks.
Alex	We're really great now. Our beat is good. Our sounds are good.
Mel	Even Carol's singing is great now.
Carol	Queenie! Queenie! I'm not Carol. I'm Queenie. Queen Bee of The Wanna Beez. Oozing glam. Oozing sweetness. Oozing nectar!
Alex	Oozing mud. That brown eye-shadow looks like mud.
Ben	Who wants another coke? Or an apple fizzy spritzer? My Dad gave me loads.
Mel	They're disgusting. No wonder he can't sell them in the pub.
Alex	They taste like old tom cats.
Carol	How do you know what a tom cat tastes like?
Ben	I know what one sounds like when it's in pain!
	[*Carol notices something on the other side of the mall.*]
Carol	Hey, don't look now but there's someone over there who looks just like Kelly Matthews off the telly.
Ben	Where?

Carol	Over there. By the Pizza Palace.
Ben	Where? I can't see anyone.
Carol	Behind the big fat man in the red shirt. Next to Woolworths.
Ben	Oh no. Nothing like Kelly Matthews. Wrong colour hair.
Mel	And Kelly Matthews doesn't wear glasses.
Alex	Never mind about Kelly fizzing Matthews! What are we going to do about the Wanna Beez? Don't you want to be in show biz?
Mel	And make a million?
Alex	And go on tour around the world?
Carol	Ooh! I'd love to go to Disney World and New York and New Zealand. I'd look great in Australia. Queenie in Queensland!
Ben	Some hope. We've practised so hard. All for nothing.
	[*A voice comes over the loud speaker system.*]
Voice	Ladies and gentlemen. Can we have your attention for a moment, please? Today is a very special day for Sheldon Shopping Mall. Today, we are thrilled to welcome the world-famous TV presenter and personality, Kelly Matthews!

Carol	Ooh! I was right! See! I told you it was Kelly Matthews.
Voice	Kelly is here for a very special reason.
Alex	To plug a new book, I bet.
Mel	They want people to buy it.
Carol	Sh! Sh! Shush!
Voice	Kelly's new show starts next month on prime time TV. It's a brand new show called Surprise Session. So here to tell you all about it, is our very own star. Please give a great welcome to Kelly Matthews!

[A bright light shines onto a small stage. Kelly Matthews runs onto it with a mike.]

Kelly	Good morning. Good morning, all you lovely people. And what a lovely morning it is, too. Now, I'm here to let you into a little secret. My new show, Surprise Session, has already started. Some of the filming has already been done. Right here in Sheldon Shopping Mall.
Carol	When?
Kelly	When? This very morning. That's when, my dear. That's the secret and that's the surprise.
Alex	What do you mean? What's going on?
Ben	Sshshsh.

Kelly	Look! Can you see all these security cameras, dotted around the mall? Well, they're always working, aren't they? Filming everybody, all the time. Well, today they've been doing two jobs at the same time. Because today they have also been making a film of all you lovely people. Zooming in on you, in secret.
Carol	Cool! Fancy that!
Mel	But that would just be boring. People wandering in and out of the shops.
Alex	Sh!
Kelly	But that's not all. There's another surprise and another secret.
Ben	I bet this is some sort of joke.
Kelly	Hidden in amongst you this morning, there are all my talent spotters. They are looking for tomorrow's pop idols. Tomorrow's telly stars, comics and soap stars.
Carol	Wow!
Kelly	My talent spotters have been listening to you. They have been listening to your jokes. They have been listening to your hopes and they have been listening to your dreams.
Alex	I don't believe it.
Mel	How could they?

Kelly	You don't believe me? Let me prove it to you! Leela! Where are you? Show yourself to our friends here in Sheldon Shopping Centre!
	[*The cleaner rips off her overall and wig to show herself as a girl in a pop-top and a mini-skirt.*]
Ben	Wow!
Carol	Ooh! Scary!
Alex	I still don't believe it. It's weird!
Kelly	And now, Curtis! Where are you? Show yourself to our friends here in Sheldon Shopping Centre!
	[*The security man rips off his uniform to show himself wearing shorts and a vest. He grins and waves.*]
Carol	Coo! I fancy him!
Kelly	And now, Scotty. Where are you? Show yourself to our friends in Sheldon Shopping Centre!
	[*The little old lady sitting on the bench with the Wanna Beez rips off her coat and wig. It is a man in drag. He waves.*]
Alex	Wow! I don't believe it!
Mel	She's been sitting here all the time. I mean *he's* been sitting here all the time.
Carol	Listening to every word we said.
Kelly	That's Scotty Brown. He's the director of my show.

[He bows to the Wanna Beez and he shakes their hands.]

Alex   Wow! I don't believe it!

Carol He was listening to every word we said.

Kelly Yes. He's been listening to every word you said.

Alex   Wow! I don't believe it!

Kelly Yes. You can believe it. We want you to come up here and play for us. *This* is your gig. Go for it!

Ben   But how do you know that we can play? How do you know if we are any good?

Kelly Your Dad e-mailed me, Ben.

Ben   My Dad's never heard us.

Kelly Yes, he has. And what's more, he's here this morning. I'll just call him on the mobile. Hello, Mr Blackwell. You can come out now.

[Dad comes out of the Pizza Palace, talking into his mobile.]

Dad   Hello, Kelly. I am here. Thanks, Kelly.

Ben   Dad!

Dad   Hello, son. I heard you rehearsing at home. And I could tell you were good. I'm more 'with it' than you think. So, one night, I came to Sheldon Village Hall. I hung around by the exit and listened to all of you.

Carol	Wow! Your Dad's cool!
Ben	I don't believe it.
Alex	I thought it was just me who didn't believe it!
Kelly	Your Dad can tell talent when he hears it.
Dad	Yes, I *can* tell talent when I hear it. And the Wanna Beez have got real talent.
Ben	Not like cats in pain?
Dad	Not a bit like cats in pain. You've got real talent.
Mel	Wow. Real talent.
Dad	So I e-mailed Kelly to tell the TV show all about you.
Alex	Wow. Real talent.
Kelly	Now, the Wanna Beez have got their first gig. Wanna Beez, this is your big chance. Alex, Ben, Carol and Mel . . . Come on up! Come up on this stage and play for all the good people in the Sheldon Shopping Centre.
Carol	Ooh! Are we going to be on the telly?
Kelly	Yes. On the telly. This is your big chance. Ladies and gentlemen, please give a very big hand to your very own Pop Idols! It's the fantastic, the great, the wonderful Wanna Beez!
Dad	Go for it, Wanna Beez!

[*People cheer and clap as the Wanna Beez go up on stage to set up and play their very first gig.*]

Kelly   Now, what are you going to sing and play for us this morning? Ben, come and tell me the name of your new single.

[*Ben turns and shouts to his Dad.*]

Ben   Dad, you're never going to believe this!

Dad   Don't tell me it's called, 'Cats in Pain'.

Ben   No. Not 'Cats in Pain'. But . . .

[*Ben goes to Kelly and whispers in her ear.*]

Kelly   Right. Ladies and gentlemen of Sheldon, please get your mobiles ready. Put on your sexy hats and give a big hand to Queenie and The Wanna Beez with their latest hit single! Would you believe it's called, 'Cool Chats in the Rain'!

[*Dad groans. Everyone cheers and waves their mobile phones in time with the music, as the Wanna Beez start to play. Carol and Mel pretend to use their mobiles while they sing to each other. Freeze.*]

'Cool Chats in the Rain' is a great song. Look out for it. It will be a number one hit soon!